D0014250

DATE DUE

GAYLORD   #3523PI   Printed in USA

Mark Zuckerberg

Facebook Creator

Other titles in the Innovators series include:

INNOVATORS

Mark Zuckerberg

Facebook Creator

ADAM **W**OOG

KIDHAVEN PRESS
A part of Gale, Cengage Learning

GALE
CENGAGE Learning™

Detroit • New York • San Francisco • New Haven, Conn • Waterville, Maine • London

GALE
CENGAGE Learning

Dedication

To Stu Witmer and Rebecca Roush, my very first friends on Facebook

© 2009 Gale, Cengage Learning

LIBRARY OF CONGRESS CATALOGING-IN-PUBLICATION DATA

Woog, Adam, 1953–
  Mark Zuckerberg, Facebook creator / by Adam Woog.
    p. cm. -- (Innovators)
  Includes bibliographical references and index.
  ISBN 978-0-7377-4566-5 (hardcover)
  1. Zuckerberg, Mark, 1984– 2. Facebook (Firm)--Juvenile literature. 3. Facebook (Electronic resource)--Juvenile literature. 4. Webmasters--United States--Biography--Juvenile literature. 5. Businesspeople--United States--Biography--Juvenile literature. 6. Online social networks--Juvenile literature. I. Title. II. Title: Facebook creator.
  HM479.Z83W66 2009
  006.7'54092--dc22
  [B]
                                                                    2009013458

KidHaven Press
27500 Drake Rd.
Farmington Hills, MI 48331

ISBN-13: 978-0-7377-4566-5
ISBN-10: 0-7377-4566-5

Printed in the United States of America
1 2 3 4 5 6 7 13 12 11 10 09

CONTENTS

The Face Behind Facebook

Mark Zuckerberg seems like a typical young man—mostly. He is in his twenties. He still has the boyish face and wide smile he had when he was a kid. He always wears the same clothes: T-shirts, hooded sweatshirts, and flip-flop sandals. He laughs a lot, and he likes rock music and movies on DVD.

But Zuckerberg is not just a typical young man. He is also the world's youngest billionaire. His personal fortune has been estimated at $1.5 billion. And he is world-famous.

An Internet Web site called Facebook is the reason. Zuckerberg created it when he was still a teenaged student at Harvard University.

Needing Computers

As its tens of millions of fans already know, Facebook is a "social-networking" tool. These fans post information about themselves, such as photos, favorite movies and music, or the schools they attend. Then they connect with friends or search for people they have lost touch with. Facebook is especially helpful if people want to do things like organize parties or tell friends what they are doing at the moment.

Zuckerberg started Facebook in 2004. It grew very quickly. Now it has more than 150 million members. It is the sixth most visited Web site in the world.

Although a billionaire, Zuckerberg prefers a comfortable, casual look with T-shirts, sandals, and jeans.

Zuckerberg is young to be a CEO (chief executive officer) of a company, especially one as big as Facebook. Being Facebook's CEO means that he is its head. As its chief, he has set many important goals for the company. One of these goals is to find ways to help people use the power of computing in the best way possible.

It is no surprise that Zuckerberg is obsessed with the power of computing. Computers have been essential to him for nearly his entire life. He says, "I need [computers] just as much as I need food."[1] This interest in computers began when Zuckerberg was just a boy.

CHAPTER 1

Discovering Computers

Mark Elliot Zuckerberg was born on May 14, 1984. He was born in White Plains, New York, a suburb of New York City. He grew up in the nearby town of Dobbs Ferry.

Zuckerberg's father, Edward, is a dentist. His mother, Karen, is a **psychiatrist**. Zuckerberg also has three sisters: Randi, Arielle, and Donna. Mark is the second oldest of the four.

He first became interested in computers in grade school. He got his first one when he was ten years old. For many kids, computers are just a way to play games or do their homework. But Zuckerberg wanted to know more and do more. He wanted to create software for the computer. Soon after he got his computer, he was writing **code** for it. He learned how to do this from a book, *C++ for Dummies*, and from talking with his friends.

Zuckerberg was therefore much more interested in computing than most people his age. In many ways, however, he led an average life. He did many things that ordinary kids do. For instance,

Unlike most kids, Zuckerberg was more interested in creating software and writing code for computers than playing games when he was young.

when he was thirteen, Zuckerberg had a **bar mitzvah**. This ceremony is common for Jewish boys when they reach that age. Zuckerberg was a big fan of the *Star Wars* movies, so his bar mitzvah party had a *Star Wars* theme.

He went to public schools for his elementary and middle school years and for his first two years of high school. Then he transferred to a prominent private school. This school was Philips Exeter Academy. It is expensive and can be difficult to get into. Zuckerberg was able to go there because he had very good grades and because his parents could afford it. Considering that both of his parents are medical professionals, it made sense that Zuckerberg would also want to be well educated.

Exeter is in New Hampshire. Zuckerberg lived in a dormitory there, since it was far from his home. He chose the school because it had advanced classes in computers and math. It also had a Latin program. Zuckerberg wanted to learn Latin because he hoped to study ancient literature.

At Exeter, he was very busy. He belonged to the math team, the science Olympiad, the band, and the Latin honors society. He also liked to **fence**. Zuckerberg excelled at this sport. In 2000, while he was still in high school, he was voted Most Valuable Player at a regional competition of the U.S. Fencing Association. Some fencing champions are very young. For example, at least two national champions have been under the age of fifteen. Still, it is quite unusual for a teenager to achieve such a high honor.

Zuckerberg transferred to the prominent private school Philips Exeter Academy when he was in high school.

Synapse

Even though he had many other interests, computers remained perhaps the most important to Zuckerberg during his high school years. He wrote a computer version of the board game Risk. And he created a Web site that let Exeter students order snacks online. One program he wrote helped people in his father's office communicate with each other. Zuckerberg also wrote a program with a friend, Adam D'Angelo. This program prompted one of their classmates, Kristopher Tillery, to recall, "They were the most advanced computer-science students at the school."[2]

Their project was a music program for MP3 players called Synapse. Synapse kept track of what people liked to listen to. Then it automatically suggested other kinds of music. That way,

At Exeter, Zuckerberg developed a music program for MP3 players that introduced users to new music that they might find interesting.

people could build digital libraries of music they liked. Essentially, the program guided users to discover music that was new to them. Zuckerberg says, "I thought, 'You know, there's really no reason why my computer shouldn't just know what I want to learn [about] next.'"[3]

The two friends posted Synapse as a free **download** on the Internet. It was a big hit. In fact, Synapse was so popular that big companies, including Microsoft and AOL, tried to buy it. They also wanted to hire its creators.

But the teenagers did not want to sell their program or get jobs. They wanted to start college. Zuckerberg got into one of the nation's top schools, Harvard University in Cambridge, Massachusetts. He started there in the fall of 2002.

Harvard

In college Zuckerberg took some computer classes, but that was not his academic focus. He majored in **psychology**. He says the combination of these two subjects, computers and psychology, seemed natural to him. He felt that computers could help people to connect better, and that this would in turn help them understand each other better.

At first, life at the university was difficult for Zuckerberg. For one thing, he was used to being one of the smartest kids in his class. But he had chosen one of America's top universities. At Harvard, he was just one of many very smart students.

Also, Zuckerberg was shy and did not make friends easily. He did not like to talk about his private life very much. Furthermore, his sarcastic sense of humor alienated some students. Spending time in his dorm room, working on writing code for new programs, was helpful, because it kept his mind busy and helped him cope with the other problems in his personal life.

Although Zuckerberg took some computer classes at Harvard University (pictured), his major was psychology.

Also, Zuckerberg found other students who were interested in computing and the same things that interested him, so he was able to make friends.

Out of class, Zuckerberg spent time in his room writing computer programs. One of these was called Coursematch. It let Harvard students see who else was in their classes. Students supplied Zuckerberg with information about the classes they were taking. Then Coursematch could use this information to make lists of classes in common.

Another project was a study guide for the final exam in a class about the history of art. Zuckerberg had been too busy with computer projects to study for the final exam. But he found a solution. He built a Web site that was a study guide for the class. He invited others to write notes on the site and use it as a resource. The site was very popular. Most of the students in the class used it and helped make it better by writing notes. It did them a lot of good. The grades for the exam that year were the highest ever for that class.

Facemash

Zuckerberg started another project in the fall of 2003, when he was nineteen. It was a site where people could see pictures of other students. It was the beginning of what would become Facebook.

He got the idea from Harvard's "facebook." This was a book the university printed to help new students learn about each

Harvard's student directory was the inspiration for Face-mash, an online site that let students see each other's photos and make comments.

other. It had photos and details about the students, such as their hometowns.

Zuckerberg created a site called Harvard Face Mash: The Process. (The name was later changed to facemash.com.) He started it one night when he was alone in his dorm room. He was sad because a girlfriend had broken up with him. Zuckerberg took his mind off his troubles by working on his new idea.

Zuckerberg **hacked** into Harvard's computer directory of students. He downloaded photographs from it. Then he invited other students to log on and comment on the photos.

The site was popular at once. Within a few hours, about 450 people had logged on. But Facemash did not last long. After a few more hours, Harvard made Zuckerberg shut it down.

The school authorities were worried about protecting the privacy of students. Also, they were angry that Zuckerberg had hacked into their computer without permission.

He got into a lot of trouble. Harvard could have **expelled** him, but the student was lucky. He got only a warning. And he was on his way to creating something much bigger.

CHAPTER 2

Launching Facebook

Soon after Harvard shut Facemash down, Zuckerberg started work on a bigger project. He called it The Facebook. ("The" was later dropped from its name.)

This site used the same idea, but it was better. With Facemash, users could only see students' pictures and post comments on the site. But with The Facebook, they could post photos of themselves, provide information, and write messages to each other.

Zuckerberg launched it on the night of February 4, 2004. It was part of his personal Web site. Zuckerberg's roommate, Dustin Moskovitz, helped him tell other students in their dormitory about The Facebook.

The new site was popular right away, and word spread to other Harvard students in other dormitories. Teachers and **alumni** also liked it. Within twenty-four hours, Facebook had about fifteen hundred members.

People continued to tell other people about it. After two weeks, the site had more than four thousand members. Olivia Ma, who was a student then, recalls, "I remember people competing to see how many 'friends' they could accumulate [gather] and how quickly, and tracking how many 'friends' they shared in common with other 'friends.'"[4]

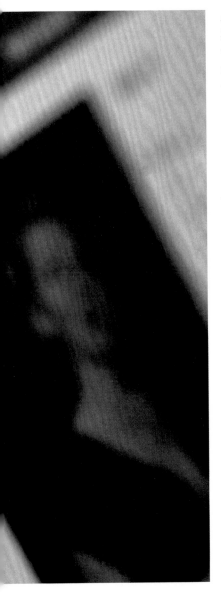

After Facemash was shut down, Zuckerberg created The Facebook, in which students could post photos of themselves, provide information, and write messages to each other.

Facebook Expands

As the site's popularity grew, it created controversy. Three other Harvard students say that they had had the original idea and that Zuckerberg had stolen it from them.

These students said they had been working on a project that used the same idea called HarvardConnection. They asked Zuckerberg to help finish it. One of the three, Tyler Winklevoss, states, "We met Mark, and we talked to him, and we thought this guy seems like a winner."[5]

Instead of helping however, the three students claim Zuckerberg secretly finished it and took the credit. He then made it public without letting the others know. This controversy still continues, and Zuckerberg continues to deny it.

In any case, Zuckerberg was able to make Facebook grow rapidly. As it got bigger, Zuckerberg decided to expand it to other schools. He asked Moskovitz to help him. Three others, Eduardo Saverin, Andrew McCollum, and Chris Hughes, also helped.

Tyler Winklevoss, left, and Cameron Winklevoss, right, who are twin brothers, and Divya Narendra sued Zuckerberg, claiming he stole their idea and took credit for it as his own.

The group started by including students from some of America's other top universities. These included Stanford, Columbia, and Yale. Then students at more schools joined. Within a few months, hundreds of thousands of people in about forty-five schools were using it.

Moving to California

Zuckerberg decided to make Facebook the basis for an entire company. In the spring of 2004, he took a **leave of absence** from Harvard so that he could work full-time on it. He wanted to start his company in Palo Alto, California.

Palo Alto is in Silicon Valley, which is the center of the computer industry in America. Zuckerberg thought it would be a good place to work. He felt that his company would do well surrounded by other computer businesses. Plus, he liked California.

The others decided to go with Zuckerberg, and his girlfriend, Priscilla Chan, joined them later. The group rented a small house on a quiet street. This was Facebook's first office.

In 2004 Zuckerberg took a leave of absence from Harvard and moved Facebook to Palo Alto, California, where several other software and computer companies are headquartered.

The group lived and worked there. They worked almost all the time. Every afternoon and night, they sat around a table in the living room with their computers. They often stayed up all night.

Having Fun

Zuckerberg also had some fun. For instance, he relaxed by watching his favorite DVDs, such as *Gladiator* and *Wedding Crashers*. He also listened to albums by bands like Green Day. And sometimes he swam in the pool behind the house.

Zuckerberg still enjoyed fencing, too. At first he practiced inside the house. But the swordplay annoyed his housemates. They made him stop.

Sometimes, the Facebook group got in trouble with the man who owned their house. He told them that the neighbors complained. He asked them not to throw furniture into the pool, talk outside after 10 P.M., or climb on the roof.

They decided to move to a nearby town, Los Altos. They rented another home there and named it Casa Facebook. (*Casa* is Spanish for "house.")

Casa Facebook was a lot like a college dormitory. The kitchen was filled with cakes, cookies, potato chips, and other snacks. The office was crammed with desks and computers. And the patio wall had green spatters all over it. These were left from the paintball games Zuckerberg and his friends liked to play.

Growing

At first, Zuckerberg did not plan to stay in California. He planned to go back to Harvard in the fall. But at the end of the summer the whole group decided to stay in California and make Facebook a full-time job for themselves. Soon after, in the

Zuckerberg attended the SXSW Film & Music Festival in Austin, Texas, to speak and to make time for fun.

fall of 2005, they made the site available to high school students as well as college students.

Within months, Facebook had 5.5 million users. About a year later, in the fall of 2006, Zuckerberg opened it up even further. Now anyone who was thirteen or older could sign up if they had a working e-mail address. Naturally, this made the number of users jump even higher. (Although Facebook still restricts membership to people thirteen and over, there are some Internet Web sites that are similar networks designed to be safe for kids.)

As the site grew, so did the need for money. Facebook was expensive to run, mostly because it needed to make heavy use of **servers**. So Zuckerberg sold part of Facebook to a company

In 2006 Zuckerberg opened up Facebook membership to anyone thirteen and older.

for $12.7 million and a smaller piece to the Microsoft Corporation. In exchange, these companies hoped to get some of Facebook's profits.

With the new money, Zuckerberg hired several more people. He was also able to move Facebook's office to downtown Palo Alto. The new office was in a big building. However, like Casa Facebook, it looked like a college dorm. It was crowded with computers. It also had plenty of room for games and food.

Zuckerberg was now a millionaire several times over. The little project that he had started for fun had become the fifth most valuable Internet company in the country. As it continued to grow, Zuckerberg learned many things from it.

CHAPTER 3

Maintaining and Growing Facebook

Zuckerberg's decision to make Facebook a full-time job meant that he could devote his talent and energy to making the site an important networking tool. Under his leadership, Facebook has been able to give people all over the world a chance to interact, connect, and reconnect. Along the way he has learned many lessons and has used them to make Facebook better.

Communication and Information

By starting and growing Facebook, Zuckerberg has learned a lot about communication. The site emphasizes how important it is to communicate by connecting and sharing information. This kind of sharing is a typical, human activity, which is why Facebook supports it. Zuckerberg comments, "It's really most natural for people to communicate through [a social network] with the people around you, friends, and business connections or whatever."[6]

Getting information is not just useful. It is also important for helping people understand each other, which helps them understand the world at large. In part, Facebook's emphasis on this idea reflects Zuckerberg's studies at Harvard in both computers and psychology. Facebook is able to combine the two, by using a high-tech tool to let people get to know each other. Zuckerberg says, "All my friends at school, we always talked about how the world would be better if there was more infor-

Facebook connects people from across the world, allowing friends and family to keep in touch regardless of where they live.

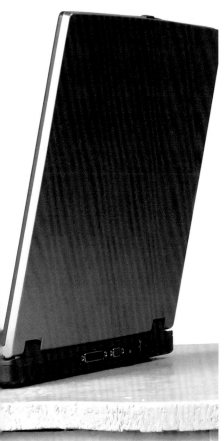

mation available, and if you could understand what was going on with other people more."[7]

Some people feel that sharing through Facebook's tens of millions of connections is all good. They say that this is because it multiplies the opportunities people have to live better, more fulfilled lives. However, some people have been critical of the site. They say that Facebook actually isolates people more, because they sit in front of computers at home instead of meeting people face-to-face.

Popularity

Facebook has been popular for a variety of reasons. One is that it has a global reach. People can connect long-distance with others whom they do not see often.

Many of Facebook's fans think that this is the most important service the site provides. Zuckerberg asserts, "Facebook helps you share more efficiently with the people you talk to all the time, your family and close friends, but I think where it really excels is helping you stay connected with the people you know but don't get to talk to that much."[8]

Another reason that the site is so popular is that it is very easy to use. It has a clean and simple design. Other networking sites, such as MySpace, have complicated and elaborate designs that some people, especially young people, like a lot. However, Facebook's page layout is more plain and uncomplicated. It does not confuse people who are not used to using computers or who do not spend a lot of time on Web sites. So Facebook appeals to people, especially adults, who do not like a lot of clutter.

Facebook Programs for Change

Facebook has hundreds of applications that are just for fun. For example, users can play games with others or send birthday cards to friends. But Facebook also has many features that are designed to make the world a better place. The site's users access features like these by going to the Applications sections of their Facebook profile pages. People are then led through the simple process of using the applications.

For example, members can use a feature called Changing the Present. When a person sends a "present" (usually a cartoon or other message) to another user, the sender is charged one dollar. But the money goes to charity. The person who sends the message can choose which group receives it.

Another feature is called Takes All Kinds. It links users with groups that support good causes. For example, people can join groups that raise money for Hurricane Katrina victims, animal rights, or cancer research. People can also start their own groups.

These programs allow individuals and companies to help both their local communities and other groups around the world. Applications such as these reflect Zuckerberg's idea that

Facebook users have the option to send virtual "gifts" to friends, such as cartoon characters, toys, and food.

a company like Facebook can make money at the same time that it creates social change or helps worthy causes. In other words, Facebook can "do good and do well."

Writer James Farrar comments that Zuckerberg seems to have learned this lesson well. Farrar says that the Facebook chief instinctively realizes the importance of combining a successful business with helping others who are in need. Farrar notes, "Zuckerberg, despite his age and inexperience, has no problem [understanding this, while many businessmen] three times his age with vast experience often fail to grasp this idea."[9]

It is likely that in the future Zuckerberg will continue to travel the path he has taken. He will continue to focus on making Facebook more widespread and on improving it. He will also work to make it a powerful tool for giving to good causes and helping make the world better.

CHAPTER 4

The Future

No one can say what will happen to Mark Zuckerberg in the future. But it is likely that he will be an important figure on the Internet for a long time. This is because Facebook is still growing fast.

Facebook now has more than 150 million active users worldwide. Furthermore, more than 150,000 people join every day. If Facebook were a country, it would be the eighth most populated nation in the world. It would have more citizens than Japan, Russia, or Nigeria.

Building Something Cool

It is likely that in the future Facebook's main purpose will stay the same. Facebook's main goal was to create a new way for people to connect with each other. In many ways, it has achieved this goal.

But the site's role in the world of communication is not over. In the future, Facebook will continue to be an important tool

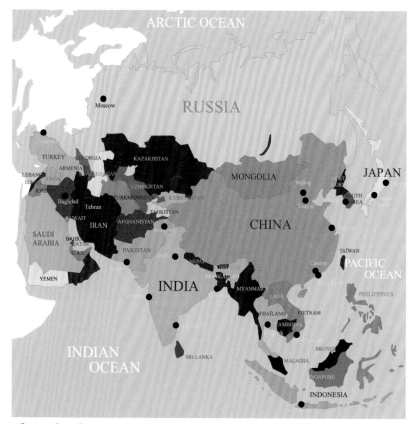

If Facebook were a country, it would be the eighth most populated nation in the world. It would have more citizens than some countries, such as Japan or Russia.

for getting information from one person or group to another. Zuckerberg comments, "Once every hundred years media changes. The last hundred years have been defined by the mass media. . . . In the next hundred years information won't be just pushed out to people, it will be shared among the millions of connections people have."[10]

Facebook will therefore continue to improve in the future, as more features are added or refined to help people share information. The site will also be improved so that it will be more entertaining and informative. Some people even feel that someday, social networking on the computer may be as popular a form of entertainment as television or the movies.

One thing that is probably not in Facebook's future is the possibility that Zuckerberg will sell it to a larger company. (This is what the creators of Facebook's biggest rival, MySpace, did.) Zuckerberg has already turned down an offer of $1 billion from Yahoo! He comments, "I'm in this to build something cool, not to get bought."[11]

Going International

Also in the future is a plan to extend Facebook to more countries. Facebook is already available in more than thirty-five different languages and in about 170 countries and territories. It will span the globe in other ways as well. For instance, in October

Egyptian Esra Abdel Fattah (right), twenty-six, hugs her mother upon being freed following a month's detention by the government for forming a group on Facebook that protested price hikes.

2008 Zuckerberg announced that the company will start an international headquarters in Dublin, Ireland. This is in addition to Facebook's main offices in Palo Alto, where about five hundred full-time employees work.

Most of these places have welcomed the site. However, some countries have kept Facebook from operating within their borders. One example is Syria. In 2007 Syrian authorities blocked Facebook in their country. Many people within Syria and in other countries have accused its leaders of blocking Facebook as a way to prevent its citizens from speaking out against the government.

The site has also been banned in many offices, both in the United States and elsewhere. Typically, this has been a business decision. The offices that have blocked the site are worried that it is too distracting. They feel that people will not work as hard if they spend too much time on Facebook.

Another problem Zuckerberg will have to work out in the future is a lawsuit. Three of his former classmates at Harvard are suing him. These are the three who say that Zuckerberg stole their idea and used much of the work they did themselves. As of early 2009, this case was still undecided.

Future Life

Zuckerberg is not afraid of working hard. However, in some ways he hopes that he will work less in the future and have more free time. He likes being his own boss, but he would like to have less responsibility in the future. In fact, he would like not to have a job at all someday. He says he will quit doing Facebook and relax when it starts to bore him.

Even as Facebook has become a powerful international company, Zuckerberg has kept his usual casual style and simple

Zuckerberg (left) was asked to attend a session at the World Economic Forum in Davos, Switzerland, in early 2007.

personal life. Although he is very rich, he does not spend much money on himself. He lives in a simple apartment that does not have many things. It is so near Zuckerberg's office that he usually walks. And he gets around the Facebook campus in a little electric golf cart.

Furthermore, Zuckerberg's workspace is just like everyone else's. And he still wears his trademark sweatshirt, T-shirt, and flip-flop sandals nearly all the time. An exception to this habit came when Zuckerberg was invited to speak at a prestigious world conference in Davos, Switzerland. On this occasion, he altered his outfit only slightly. He jokes, "It was great. I wore shoes."[12]

With or without his shoes, Zuckerberg does not plan to retire soon. He asserts, "Facebook is really not a short-term thing——it's a 10, 15, 20-year thing."[13]

He is, after all, still very young. In fact, he is so young that some people wonder if he will be able to continue being the CEO of a huge company. In any case, there is little doubt that Mark Zuckerberg will continue in the future to develop Facebook to its full potential.

Fun Facts About Mark Zuckerberg and Facebook

- Facebook has more than 150 million members.

- It is the sixth most visited Web site in the world.

- About 70 million users—roughly half of the site's members—visit it on a daily basis.

- More than 20 million active user groups exist on the site. A user group is a group of people with shared interests.

- Facebook started out being just for college students. Now its members include anyone over thirteen. Hundreds of thousands of them are over sixty-five years of age.

- Mark Zuckerberg's sister Randi works in the marketing department at Facebook.

- Facebook gets more hits per day than any other social-networking site.

- Facebook users around the world spend a total of more than 3 billion minutes on it every day.

- The average Facebook member has one hundred friends on the site.

- Facebook is the top photo-sharing site in the world. More than 800 million photos are uploaded to the site every month.

- The daily number of photos uploaded is over 14 million. More than 4 billion photos have been uploaded so far in total.

- More than 5 million videos are uploaded every month on Facebook.

- More than 20 million individual pieces of content (Web links, news stories, **blog** posts, notes, photos, etc.) are shared on the site every month.

- More than 2 million events, such as parties, are created every month on Facebook.

- Facebook is translated into more than thirty-five languages. Sixty more are still in development.

- Facebook can be found in about 170 countries and territories around the world.

- About 70 percent of all Facebook users are outside the United States.

- People who work in the Facebook offices can get three catered meals a day, free laundry and dry cleaning, and many other perks (benefits).

- Zuckerberg has no cavities (his dad is a dentist).

- Harvard University lets students take off as much time as they wish before starting classes again. Bill Gates dropped out of Harvard to start Microsoft. He encouraged Zuckerberg to do the same when he wanted to start Facebook. They are Harvard's most famous dropouts.

NOTES

Introduction: The Face Behind Facebook

1. Quoted in Kevin J. Feeney, "Business, Casual," *Harvard Crimson*, February 24, 2005. www.thecrimson.com/article .aspx?ref=505938.

Chapter One: Discovering Computers

2. Quoted in Claire Hoffman, "The Battle for Facebook," *Rolling Stone*, June 26, 2008. www.rollingstone.com/news/ story/21129 674/the_battle_for_facebook/2.

3. Quoted in Michael M. Grynbaum, "Mark E. Zuckerberg '06: The Whiz Behind thefacebook.com," *Harvard Crimson*, June 10, 2004. www.thecrimson.com/article.aspx?ref=502875.

Chapter Two: Launching Facebook

4. Quoted in John Cassidy, "Me Media," *New Yorker*, May 15, 2006. http://archives.newyorker.com/default.aspx?iid=1514 9& startpage=page0000052.

5. Quoted in Cassidy, "Me Media."

Chapter Three: Maintaining and Growing Facebook

6. Quoted in Online Community Report, "The Social Graph." www.ocreport.com/index.php?url=archives/258-The-Social- Graph-A-Conversation-with-Marc-Smith-from-Microsoft- Research.html&serendipity%5Bcview%5D=linear.

7. Quoted in Simon Garfield, "Facebook Founder Mark Zuckerberg —24-Year-Old with So Many Friends." *San Francisco Sentinel*, November 22, 2008.

8. Quoted in Garfield, "Facebook Founder Mark Zuckerberg—24-Year-Old with So Many Friends."

9. James Farrar, "Facebook: Revolution, Weed and Philanthropy." ZDNet, March 21, 2008. http://blogs.zdnet.com/sustainability/?p=118.

Chapter Four: The Future

10. Quoted in MarketingWeb, "Facebook Points the Way for Future Marketing," November 20, 2007. www.marketingweb.co.za/marketingweb/view/marketingweb/en/page72308?oid=97017&sn=Marketingweb+detail.

11. Quoted in CNNMoney.com, "Facebook Stares Down Success," November 28, 2005. http://money.cnn.com/magazines/fortune/fortune_archive/2005/11/28/8361945/index.htm.

12. Quoted in Ellen McGirt, "Facebook's Mark Zuckerberg: Hacker. Dropout. CEO," *FastCompany*, October 17, 2008. www.fastcompany.com/magazine/115/open_features-hacker-dropout-ceo.html.

13. Quoted in Garfield, "Facebook Founder Mark Zuckerberg—24-Year-Old with So Many Friends."

GLOSSARY

alumni: Graduates of a college or university.

bar mitzvah: A ceremony held for Jewish boys at the age of thirteen. (The ceremony for girls is called a bat mitzvah.)

blog: Short for *Weblog*; personal essays and other writings for Web sites.

download: Information such as pictures that can be brought from the Internet onto a computer. The opposite is an upload.

code: A system of symbols written to create instructions for a computer program.

expelled: Forced to leave. Students can be expelled from schools for breaking laws.

fence: To compete with swords in the sport of fencing.

hacked: To hack is to have broken into a computer system. This is almost always illegal.

leave of absence: A temporary period away from a job or school. Typically, a person taking a leave of absence returns to the same job or school.

psychiatrist: A medical doctor who specializes in the treatment of mental illness.

psychology: The science of studying mental processes. People who specialize in this field are called psychologists. They typically have doctorate degrees (PhDs), but they are not medical doctors.

servers: Computers that provide services used by other computers. For example, Web servers gather and help maintain Web pages.

FOR FURTHER EXPLORATION

Web Sites

BrainPOP (www.brainpop.com/technology/computersandinter net/internet/preview.weml). Information about how the Internet connects people and groups.

Facebook for Kids (www.facebookforkids.com). A site similar to Facebook, but just for kids. It is designed to be easy and safe for them to use. It is not part of Facebook.com.

DVDs

CBS/Lesley Stahl, "The Face Behind Facebook," *60 Minutes*. New York: CBS, 2008. A thirteen-minute profile and interview with Zuckerberg. It aired on the TV show *60 Minutes* on January 13, 2008.

Oxford Scientific Films/John Heilemann, *Internet True History*. Oxford, England: Oxford Scientific Films, 2008. A three-hour documentary that aired on the Discovery Channel. Part of it focuses on Mark Zuckerberg and Facebook.

INDEX

PICTURE CREDITS

Cover photo: Sean Gallup/Getty Images

AFP/Getty Images, 33

AP Images, 20, 35

Image copyright Noam Armonn, 2009. User under license from Shutterstock.com, 26–27

© Joe Bird/Alamy, 12

Image copyright Miodrag Gajic, 2009. User under license from Shutterstock.com, 24

Chris Jackson/Getty Images, 18–19

Image copyright Yegor Korzh, 2009. User under license from Shutterstock.com, 15

David McNew/Getty Images, 21

Gary Miller/FilmMagic/Getty Images, 23

Image copyright Martine Oger, 2009. User under license from Shutterstock.com, 32

© Royalty-Free/Corbis, 10

© Philip Scalia/Alamy, 11

Used under license from Shutterstock.com, 29

Image copyright Pattie Steib, 2009. User under license from Shutterstock.com, 14

© Kimberly White/Reuters/Corbis, 7

About the Author

Adam Woog has written many books for adults, young adults, and children. He is especially interested in history and biography. Woog lives in his hometown, Seattle, Washington, with his wife and their daughter.